Angels

They Are Really Real

Mary McGee

authorHOUSE®

AuthorHouse™
1663 Liberty Drive
Bloomington, IN 47403
www.authorhouse.com
Phone: 1 (800) 839-8640

Published by AuthorHouse   10/12/2015

Library of Congress Control Number: 2015910434

ISBN: 978-1-5049-2076-6 (sc)
ISBN: 978-1-5049-2075-9 (e)

KJV

*Scripture quotations marked KJV are from the Holy Bible, King James Version
(Authorized Version). First published in 1611. Quoted from the KJV Classic
Reference Bible, Copyright © 1983 by The Zondervan Corporation.*

Print information available on the last page.

*Any people depicted in stock imagery provided by Thinkstock are models,
and such images are being used for illustrative purposes only.
Certain stock imagery © Thinkstock.*

This book is printed on acid-free paper.

Contents

My Prayer

Most Holy, righteous, and faithful God. Lord I praise your name; I glorify your holy name. I thank you God for your son Jesus, and his angels that you sent to watch over us, both day and night. Lord Jesus, I pray that your people will learn more about your angel servants and learn to appreciate them, love them and acknowledge their presence in their lives. Jesus, open your people mind so they may learn about what the purpose your heavenly host is to them and let them remember what your word says; "and in all your getting get an understanding of My word". Thanking you in advance in Jesus name, Amen.

Proverbs 4:7

Scripture Reading

Exodus 23:20

I am sending an Angel ahead of you.

Psalm 34:7

The angel of Lord encampeth
round them that fear him,
and delivereth them.

Isaiah 6:1-2-3

In the year that King Uzziah died, I saw the Lord sitting on a throne, high and lifted up, and the train of His *robe* filled the temple. [2] Above it stood seraphim; each one had six wings: with two he covered his face, with two he covered his feet, and with two he flew. [3] And one cried to another and said: "Holy, Holy, Holy *is* the LORD of hosts; The whole earth *is* full of His glory.

Why I Wrote This Book

Why would I write a book on Angels? What possible value is there in reading the discussion of angels? Some think that angels were just a saying –some others think that angels existed and that everybody had one. Well, I have come to know that angels do exist. The devil, however, would rather you disbelieve that they do. You can't let your mind stay focused on the myth that angels don't exist because there is so much in the Bible that supports the real truth about God's angels. We all know that God is omnipotent; God has all power. God has provided his people with faith, and power over the enemy. You must hold on to God's word and study the word, so that you will know what God say's about angels and their existence. God teaches us also not to be deceived nor are we to be intimidated.

I believe that angels exist because God said they would watch over us day and night. I believe if God said it then it is true because God can not lie. If you are a Holy Saint I Know You Can Fell Their Presence with you. God has countless number of angels to go to any part of the world at his command, to protect and take charge over his people and also to ward off danger. Angels are there to ward off satan when he tries to steal your joy and the struggles of life. When the angels stand guard over you, know that Jesus is right there. I am a witness that they have been there for me.

God speaks about angels before man was made. If you must study His word on angels (Hebrews 1:13) then you will know when they are in your presence. In the upcoming chapters, I will be reflect on the spiritual experiences of my daughter, my son and of myself concerning angels. I hope that I can answer some of your questions which will satisfy your curiosity about God's angels and their purposes here on earth. Additionally, take time to reexamine your thoughts. Are you able to remember the last time you really stopped to thank God for the angel that watches over you, and your loved ones?

About the Author

Mary McGee was born in Kinston, North Carolina, one of thirteen children to Mr. and Mrs. Louis and Ruth Simmons. Needless to say she was surrounded by love. When she graduated from high school she moved to Washington, District of Columbia away from her loved ones and started a life in the city. She found a church that met all of her spiritual needs. She was born again and filled with God's Holy Spirit. She's married and have a son, a daughter and two-step-children. She is a 1st Lady, a Deaconess, an Intercessor, and she sing in her church choir. Mary is a Christian counselor and love what she does. She also owns a Day Care facility. Writing is something she loves to do, and the Lord wouldn't limit her to only tell His people about His goodness, His angels and His blessings. She is a true praiser, and she loves the Lord. She now resides in Fort Washington, Maryland.

Angels

So you ask-What are angels? Well, angels are servants that can appear and remain invisible as they perform tasks. The word angel comes from the Greek word angelos which means messenger. (Hebrews 1:4) They are assigned different tasks by the Lord Jesus Christ. Many Christians think that angels of God are present for His people, and that we can take comfort in knowing with the host of angels around us, we are not alone.

Angels were the first to be created and is the highest in rank of all creation; although they are highly ranked, they are not above God. They are servants and are not equal to God. Remember, they are angels and must not be worshipped, only God is in that divine order, He and He alone deserves and should get our praise.

God is the creator; angels are in heaven to perform certain duties for Him, such as warning His people in spirit and delivering messages from the Creator on the throne to the earth below. Angels are ranked as follow: (from the highest to the lowest) Seraphim, Cherubim, Thrones dominions, Virtues, Powers, Principalities, Archangels and Angels. Colossians: 1:11-16, Colossians: 17-19.

God created the universe and the earth. The angels rejoiced with God, Job: 38:4-7. The angels rejoiced over His creation of the earth, thereby proving the angels were here before man was made by God. However, the Bible does not tell us how long after the creation of angels, God created man.

There are three heavens mentioned in the Bible. The first heaven is the sky and its atmosphere and surroundings. The second heaven is the universe, what we now call the outer space, and the third heaven is where we believe God and His angels resides in all His glory. Revelation: 21:1-5.

It is so hard sometimes to get people to believe in the brighter side of the unknown and unseen, but it is so easy for people to believe in the dark side of the unseen world. (I speak of God's angels from the brighter side and demon angels from the dark side). God's angels are sent here to guard and protect us from the dark side.

Chapter 1
God's Secret Agent
Angel Visitation

On this cold winter day in January, I decided to put on paper the words that were on my mind. I am a member of a large congregation that believes in Jesus Christ and the word. We are a church that also believes in angels. I remember our revival that lasted two weeks because the anointing was so high.

The Bishop was delivering the word and asked everybody to stand and just give God some praise because "He is still here". The anointing was so high, the church seemed to fill with smoke. As we continued to praise God, the speaker of the night came forth with a prophecy and said, "the Lord said that you all should stand and praise him" because you are being visited by ministering angels. Get up and worship Him! The saints were running around the church, some were on their knees; some were crying out to the Lord while some others were speaking in a heavenly language.

I looked up near the balcony, and I saw an angel

flying with twinkling lights. It was an awesome sight and so pretty that words can't explain how I felt. The saints were at the church from 5:00 p.m. until the next morning; needless to say we were right back at service at 5:00 p.m., that day, so we could get a seat. The church was filled every night; the saints were hungry for the word. The visiting speaker opened the service that night by saying that we will never be the same after last night's service because we had been really visited by angels. The praise team began to sing uplifting and anointing hymns that ushered in the presence of the Lord.

Visitation

I was at church for service the next week and each night was just awesome; each night the congregation witnessed a different experience! We were on such a spiritual high, and we continued to feel the presence of the Holy Ghost well into the month of February. At our regular prayer services, a lot of people were set free, filled with the Holy Ghost, and healed. People were coming from far and near just to get to our church because they heard about the sightings, the anointing that had fallen upon the sons and daughters of Christ each and every night.

I saw the Bishop pray for hundreds of people on Sunday and Tuesday nights services. People were coming to receive the Holy Ghost, which is extremely important. If a person is saved and filled with the Holy Ghost, that person will see all the angels and the creator of them, Jesus Christ when we are taken home to live with Him.

On Sunday mornings, there would always be about two thousand worshippers at 8:00 a.m. and the 11:00 a.m. service. The praise team and minister of music were ready to usher in the spirit of the Lord. All the Bishop needed to do was get into the word. His text for one of the services was "How Many of You Have Your Bibles"? Raise them up so I can see them. Greet your neighbor with a Holy Ghost hug and give the Lord praise; now let's get ready for the word. He would always tell us to read our Bible and stay prayed up because we never know when we might experience another visitation by an angel.

Angels Visitation

Well, we were into the last few nights of the revival, and we were now being called the soul saving center. Bishop's famous saying was "You catch them and bring them in, and I will fry them" (smile). The Lord was just blessing His people every night, and we were still on our 4 -day fast as well, so we were in the clouds any way. We just love to worship the Lord.

One Sunday morning, service had just begun, and the praise team was about to start the worship service which sets the tone for the Lord to come in- not that He wasn't already there; but we could feel that there was something in the air that wasn't the norm. Songs were sung; then when it came time to pray, the minister prayed. The saints started crying and praying like never before. The praise team continued to sing while the saints cooled down a little, well those that could anyway.

Now it's time for the message I said to myself, "I don't know about this, I don't know how he is going to preach with the anointing this high". The Bishop stood up, walked to the roster and stood there for a moment. Then he started jumping up and down saying, You better praise God. The time is now. He is here Praise Him! Can't you feel him? "He is here", the saints were going off with praise, and it didn't take much at this time because they were already prayed up. The church was filled from the front to the back, even the chairs in aisle.

Bishop stopped again and just looked at the people including the ones in the balcony and smiled. He said "Jesus and His angels are here. Praise Him!" He wasn't a man that danced, but he would always just jump up and down. Needless to say, the saints went into a high praise, the angels were up near the balcony, you could see the twinkling of lights and smoke filled the church again. The lights were twinkling as the angels were flying across the balcony. Also, at the side of the church up near the ceiling, we could see the twinkling of lights. It was just amazing!

Bishop was preparing to deliver the sermon the best he could because he was so filled with the anointing that he could hardly control himself. At the same time, the saints were just trying to calm each other down, enough to hear the word that was about to come forth. Finally the Bishop stopped and said; "There is about to be a change in service", God's angels are in this place and anyone who wants to be healed come to the altar right now. Come now!"

Bishop came down and started to lay hands on the people at the altar and when he finished with them, he preceded to walk the aisle calling out the people that needed prayer and those that needed to be saved. There were people on the floor in the aisle and up front at the altar, I think he prayed for everybody that morning; he even went out of the sanctuary into the foyer still laying hands on people. When he came back into the sanctuary he looked different. We could see, the anointing on him. He went back to the pulpit and lifted his hands up and started to praise the Lord and as I looked up I saw a giant angel, big and tall standing behind him with a sword and shield in his hand. I thought the first visitation was just awesome, but this second one was extremely spiritual and peaceful; he was just standing there as if he had been sent by God to show His approval, and that He was pleased with the praise from the Bishop and us.

God's angels came to watch over the Bishop because angels are the representatives of God sent from heaven to visit and take messages to and from His people. The angel stood behind the Bishop as if he wanted to say "I got your back Bishop", God is well pleased with your praise, your worship, and the praises of the people.

Angels are Created Beings

The Bible state that Angels are like man created by God, there were no angels at one time, they did not exist. There was nothing but the Triune of God: the father in Colossians 1:16 states that by him were all things created, in heaven and that is in the earth, visible and invisible.

The angels indeed were among the invisible things are created by God. This creator Jesus was before all things and by him all things consist, (Colossians 1:17 & 4:18). The angels would not have existed if the creator who is Jesus the Almighty God had not sustained them, by almighty power.

Angels have the ability to change their appearance and move in a flash from heaven to earth at the command of God.

Reflections

_____

_____

_____

_____

_____

_____

_____

_____

_____

_____

Reflections

_____

_____

_____

_____

_____

_____

_____

_____

_____

_____

_____

Reflections

_____

_____

_____

_____

_____

_____

_____

_____

_____

_____

_____

Chapter 2

Angels are Really Real

Chapter 2-Angels are Really Real

The Bible tell us about angels and there visitations before we arrived here on earth. When God created man, the angels were already here; they are God's glory. The angel announced the birth of Jesus Christ. Angels are spirits, and there are several different spiritual beings that are angels. There are cherubs, sometimes called messengers and angels.

These beings are real; they are forever present in our lives in time of trouble. Read the following account that shows the manifestation of an angel that gave my daughter comfort and assurance when she needed it most.

While I was at brunch with my friends, the Lord spoke to me and said, "Go home now." I looked at my friends, and they looked at me and asked me if I were alright? I said, "Yes, I think so." I heard the same words again. "Go home now." I didn't wait any longer; I got up and told my friends that I had to go right now. "I must get home." As I reached my house, I went into my bedroom, and the phone rang. It was the county police captain. He said, "You must get to the emergency room right away. Your daughter has been in a car accident, and she is being Medevac to the hospital." He stated that she was in critical condition. I asked him where were my grandsons? He said, they are alright. "He said they were in the ambulance, and the other four people involved are in the ambulance, but come quickly." (Ain't God Good!)

If you stay with God and live your life for Jesus, get filled with His precious gift of the Holy Ghost. He will warn you of danger and other things because Jesus and His angels will stand guard over you. God will speak to you.

My daughter, along with two of her girlfriends, and three small children were involved in a car accident on a Sunday after the morning service. They decided to go get something to eat before coming back to the evening service. A car hit them head on. The young man that hit them was driving a stolen car, and he was also running from the police. Some victims were sent to the hospital by ambulance, but my daughter was flown to the hospital because her condition was more serious than the other four people that were in the back seat of the car. One person was released the next day; another one that had a broken hip was released within a week. My daughter, however, stayed in the hospital for about four months and had to have four surgeries. Her body had been severely fractured, so severe, one surgery took twelve hours to put one side of her body back to gather again and another surgery took sixteen hours to do the right side back together. Ain't God good?

I thank God my daughter was saved and was trying to take her friends to church to get them saved. As my daughter arrived at the hospital, the doctor and nurses were waiting. They rushed to her and said, "Let's get her to surgery now"! They were concerned because she had two broken thigh bones that could puncture or cut an artery, which would cause her to bleed to death. Before they could get inside to stop the bleeding, another helicopter arrived with a special surgeon, the only one who could do the procedure she needed. I was allowed into the room while the surgeon was examing my daughter; she was in and out of consciousness as the doctor checked her legs. One of the nurses said, "I will get her ready for surgery" and proceeded to cut a green bracelet off her ankle. My daughter woke up long enough to say, "No don't cut that leave it on." The anklet read (I Love Jesus). The doctor asked, Is your daughter saved? I said Yes, she is. He said, I am too. That bracelet is keeping her alive. Don't take it off her. God sent me here. (Ain't God Good!)

Once in her room, my daughter asked me about "the lady" at the foot of the bed. Another time, she asked if "the lady" could go with her for x-rays and surgery? She also told me that "the lady" had been in the helicopter with her. I was certain "the lady" was an angel. My daughter would always say to me, "Mom, the lady is here. She was in the room when I had the other surgeries. Is she a friend of yours?" I couldn't see the angel because she had been assigned to my daughter, but I said, "Yes."

While waiting, she wanted to know where her friends and her son were? I explained to her that they were in different rooms and that her son Jerelle had scrapes and bruises, but none of his bones had been broken. Her girlfriend had been admitted with a broken leg, and the other three were in different rooms.

I continued to pray for her and I called my family and friends at the church to let them know her status. My daughter was so weak until I couldn't leave her for a moment. During the surgery, the doctor had to put a rod in her hip because they found out the she wouldn't be able to stand up without it. By this time, I was in complete tears because she already had rods in her thighs and in her lower legs. Now, they had to go back in and correct the hip bones on the right side so that she could stand up when she was able.

I thank God that she was saved and covered by His blood and by Jesus. She went through the hip surgery fine. Her friends went to rehabilitation and therapy. My daughter spent months in the hospital. The doctors would look at her and smile because they could not believe that she was still with us. She had been broken up so badly, they gave her little chances of living, but the God I serve can do anything but fail. When man gave up, Jesus sent an angel. My daughter is doing well. Angels are really real!!!

I think the type of experiences that my daughter had with her angel is unspeakable. A person just cannot find the words to describe such life changing and life giving experiences. Once he/she has had an encounter with an angel whether it brings healing, conversion, salvation, guidance, a warning or comfort. I urge you if you haven't been there, you should pray to the Lord that you get to experience a conscience encounter with His angels. We must know that the word says that angels come in different forms, lights and in human forms; therefore, we must believe the word. When your spirit connects with God's spirit and his angelic host of angels that will be an awesome honor and a mighty blessing.

Where Do Angel Live?

Angels live in heaven with God. If you read the Bible and search the scripture, you will find in Genesis 1:1-3, which states… "In the beginning God created the heaven and the earth". The word heaven is interpreted as heaven in the Hebrews language. That's what Paul states when he said he was caught up in the third heaven (2nd Corinthians 2:2) which means that there was a first and a second heaven as well as the third heaven, and we do know that it is not in our universe according to the Bible. This could be where the Angels get their rankings, their degrees, and their stations. This is where they reside with God in the heavenly city, and He assigns the angels their assignments to be carried out to His people. Angels are transformed to their surrounding, such as being clothed to cover their spirits while carrying out God's commands here on earth in certain insanities.

Your Spirit and Angel's Connection

The sighting of the angels was something that I will never forget and the joy and the peace that comes with that moment is indescribable. I say you must let go of yourself and let God take you to this place in Him. Bishop would always tell us about the spirit realm and the Holy place; I see just what he meant now, but when talking about angels, he would just laugh. What would cause the lack of words?

I think that type of experience is just unspeakable. A person just can't find the words to describe such a life changing experience. I urge you if you haven't been there, you should pray to the Lord that you get to experience a conscience encounter with His angels. We must know that the word says that angels come in different forms, lights, and in human forms; therefore, we must believe the word.

When your spirit connects with God's spirit and His angelic host of angels that will be an awesome honor and a might blessing.

Reflections

_____

_____

_____

_____

_____

_____

_____

_____

_____

_____

Reflections

_____

_____

_____

_____

_____

_____

_____

_____

_____

_____

_____

Reflections

Chapter 3

Angel Sent to Protect You

On this sunny morning in July, I was praying and giving God His glory for all He has done. I was in my zone (if you know what I mean) when the Lord said to me, "Tell Jr. to stay off the bike today". I said, "Lord what did You say"? The Lord said, "Tell Jr. to stay off the bike today". I thanked the Lord, and the Holy Ghost for warning me about what was going to happen. I treasure the relationship that I have with the Lord especially when He speaks to me.

As I got up off my knees I began calling for my son to warn him about the motor bike and not to ride it today. We usually talk early in the morning (Jr. is an early riser); we laugh and talk about how I am still asleep at seven o'clock. He will say, "Mom I've been up since five o'clock. You alright"? He would say a few more words and ask if I needed anything. I will call you later…love you Mom and off the phone he goes.

Well, on this morning, I couldn't find him. I was getting a little concerned about him because when the Lord speaks, I listen. I know not to take it lightly so I started calling around for him. I started walking back and forth until my daughter called. She is also an early person, but she gives me time to get up. I asked her if she heard from her brother and she replied, Yes mom. They are all riding their new motorbikes today. They called and said they would be out riding all day; because they were all off from work that day. I am sure Mom that he will call you later; they are supposed to meet some other bikers from out of town. She said, "Mom I'm sure he will call you when they make a stop to eat or gas up".

I asked my daughter to continue to call her brother until you get him and that if she reached him, tell him to call me right away and to get off that motorcycle.

Well, as the day went on, and I heard nothing from him, I could only trust the Lord to take care of him and dispatch his guardian angels to be at his side. His father called to say he would be fine and he would call me back if anything was wrong; none of them have their cell phones on them when they are riding their bikes. This was a very long day of waiting for a phone call. I called a couple of my friends to pray for him as we chatted during the day about our children, especially our boys which seem to think that they have it all together.

So I just kept on praying day and night. "Lord, watch over my son. Cover him with your blood". My son would usually call me to keep a check on whether I was at home and to let me know his destination. Well, needless to say, I decided to calm down and trust the Lord for His keepsake. It was a beautiful day outside for a ride if a person had a day off and also had a new motorcycle. Yes, he and three of his friends had new motorcycles.

Riding their bikes was their passion; it was their recreation. They rode every chance they could; they all had different type of jobs. My son is a manager for his father's bus company. One of the girls is a fantastic singer for her church, and they were good people with different backgrounds.

About eight o'clock that evening my daughter called to say he was on his way home and she would talk to us later. He told her to call and tell me that, he would call me when he got home but my phone had gone dead. I was still praying and thanking the Lord for what He has already done. An hour later one of the riders called my daughter to let her know that they had to stop again for her brother, because his hand was hurting really bad but they would be there soon. My daughter said Ok. Will you all be coming to my house? and the guys said "Yes". All of them were going to my daughter's house. The next phone call was a half hour later from one of the girls to my daughter. "Lisa come over quickly; your brother fell off his motorcycle and is in the street. Call your mother and father and come quickly we have already called the ambulance". They were about five blocks away from her house coming in from 295 into the city before he fell (Ain't God Good!) He could have fallen out there on 295 where he could have been hit by several cars but God kept him until he reached the city and on a street where there was little or no traffic. The Angels were with him!

My daughter got to him before he was moved from where he had fallen. He rolled about fifty feet and ended up under a cab. His friends had to pull him from under the cab; one of the biker's stopped the cab before he moved his car to let him know that my son was under the car, when my daughter got there, the medics were just pulling up. One of the girls that was riding with him was on her knees praying and talking to God-everyone was in shock. My daughter said her brother was just lying in the street shaking all over really bad. The paramedics started to do what they do and said which hospital they were taking him to and off they went. (Ain't God Good!)

Later, I was talking with the girls and they were crying. One of them told me that she was praying for him at the scene. When the paramedics got him to the hospital, she said he had been rolling in the street like he was a paper bag. She said he went one way and the bike went the other way. That was the angels taking charge over him, he told me the next morning the only thing he remembered was the sharp pain in his hand as he started to lean off the motorcycle. He said it seemed like someone just lifted him off the bike and went with him down to the ground, and he ended up floating down the street. He said, "Mommy do you know that I am suppose to be dead? But someone was out there when I fell; I know there were angels that took me off that motorcycle and carried me down the street so I wouldn't get killed. I know I was supposed to be dead; it was God's grace and mercy that saved me that day and my guardian angel which was there. My angel kept me from getting all broken up; I suffered a stroke on the right side of my body while riding the motorcycle.

The next day after all the test were done including x-rays, the doctor told him "You must have had someone upstairs watching over you because it is a miracle that you are not dead, young man" You have no broken bones and no internal injuries. He had a stroke while riding the motorcycle; that's why he fell off his bike. My son knows just how the Holy Ghost works, and what the power of much prayer really means. I told him about the saints, his friend and I praying for him. The Lord will use him and keep him. We just completed a twenty- one day fast so I was fasting and praying for my son. God is so awesome, I thank God for my son's life, for his guardian angels watching over him, and for always being present in his life.

You must pray for and over your children, always. We think sometimes that when they get older, that they are able to pray for themselves, but they can't always do that. There is nothing like a mother's prayer; I prayed for my son that he would make it through after the motorcycle accident and the stroke.

And he did, with the prayers of the saints and by the grace of God. I also prayed for my daughter, that she would make it through after her car accident. One of the Elder's at my church went with me to the hospital when my daughter was in ICU. He told her that she would live and not die, he also told her that she would walk again. He is an anointed and dedicated man of God; he means what he says and says what he means. He was always at the hospital with me visiting my daughter, visiting and giving us encouragement. He baptized my son, and my grandson. My son tells me all the time that he knows without God being a fence around him, that it could have been the other way. He said he knows he should have been dead, and that he knew I had to have been praying for him. He is so grateful to God for sparing his life, after a fall like that and sliding a whole block and ending up under a car. He knows that it was nobody but God and His angels. Parents continue to pray for your children, family members and church family. God hears your prayers and his heavenly host of angels are ready to be dispatched to all four corners of the earth at God's command.

Lord Jesus, I thank you for your presence in our lives, and for your ministering angels that come to share in the sunrise which you sent to bless us in theses revival services. Thank you for the soul that was washed and filled; thank you for your anointing and Lord Jesus thank you for the man of God in this house.

Amen

Do Angels Take Forms?

Well, let's see what the Bible says. The word says that angels appeared as shining lights that sparkle in the midair, so bright that when you see them you say that it must be angels. They appear dressed in white (Rev. 4-4). Regular people in the Bible refer to them as giants; angels also appear in human form as warriors or as watchmen that guard over ordinary men and women and can take on different forms and appearances as the word reveals as the Lord uses them in different places.

God can use anyone or anything. For instance, he used men in the Bible, they appeared to Abraham, as being a man of God a Theophany.

An angel took form as regular men and appeared to Lot in the City of Sodom. (Gen. 19:1-13) The angel of the Lord appeared as a flaming bush and spoke to Moses (Acts 7:30); so Angels take on whatever form the Lord decides to use after all He is God Almighty and He has all the power.

They were guards at the gate in man form (Rev. 21-22).

Angel of the Lord

The Bible speaks of the angels of the Lord being Jesus himself in angel form because no one could see Jesus and live. The Bible says that the angel of the Lord being God himself. Bible scholars say that He was Jesus in the Old Testament and he appeared to people. Why would you not be able to see him as the living God and live? The angel of the Lord was seen by many people with a sword and shield of judgment.

Many people saw him several times. In (Gen. 16-7-13) Hagar that was being mistreated as a mistress saw the angel of the Lord. He appeared and told her he would add to her seed exceedingly and that God had heard her cry of affliction. No one has the power to take or give life but God himself.

Hagar also saw the angel of the Lord again in (Gen. 21-16-18). This time she was just down and out, and she and her son were without water and food in the wilderness. She hid her son under a bush and they sat there waiting to die. The baby just kept on crying and crying until the angel of the Lord called out to her and said that God heard the child crying and her prayers. The angel told her what to do and that her son would be a great nation.

Reflections

_____

_____

_____

_____

_____

_____

_____

_____

_____

_____

_____

Reflections

_____

_____

_____

_____

_____

_____

_____

_____

_____

_____

_____

Reflections

_____

_____

_____

_____

_____

_____

_____

_____

_____

Chapter 4

Angel's Guard Over You

My day started early this morning, I was feeling kind of sad about going on a job interview because something just didn't feel right. A friend had recommended me for this position. Well, I had been on two interviews and met with the owner and some of the associates. Today, I was supposed to go to the actual site where I was to work. The Lord had fully warned me and sent me messages not to take the job, but being disobedient to the spirit, I said I would go and just see about it. The first interview was local but at an inconvient time and place. I got to the interview and had to wait for an hour before anyone was able to see me. That delay didn't go well with me, but during the interview, they just loved me and asked if I could meet with the site manager and the owner.

I was called for the third interview a few days later; I was still not feeling good about the job and I heard a little voice saying, "Don't go it's not for you;" therefore I didn't call them back to say ok right away, and after all of the circumstances surrounding this job, I ended up declining the job offer.

Let me go back a bit, when I got up in the morning of the third interview, while I was trying to get ready, I was hindered by many difficulties. Preparing myself was the hardest thing to do. I finally had to stop and pray, I asked the Lord. What is it? What are you trying to tell me or warn me about this job? You know the Holy Spirit will warn you about unforeseen things. After getting dressed and sitting down and praying, I anointed my head, hands and feet before leaving the house. I heard a voice say, Anoint yourself if you have to go. This was a little strange, but I never question what the Lord says to do. I got into my car and headed for my destination; I didn't want to be late, but as the Lord would have it when I arrived, the manager had been called to another property. Consequently, the interview had been moved to the other site about ten miles away. I was so uptight and really didn't want to drive that far in the rain. I kept hearing a voice say "Don't go" as I was driving down the street from the first site.

I was behind several cars and on the right side of the hill, rocks and mud started sliding down onto the road. The car in front of me stopped his car immediately; which caused me to hit the car in front of me. The driver said he couldn't see anything in front of him, and that's why he stopped suddenly. Incredibly, the car in front of him had also stopped suddenly, so he hit it. No one was hurt, but the couple in the first car was about 70 years old so their reflexes were not that good. They were a cute couple on their way to a doctor's appointment; I guess I was the worst off. The gentlemen I hit came to me and asked me if I was alright and if he could call someone for me?

My daughter got there before the ambulance did; my car was really messed up in the front, so much so that I couldn't even get my car door open. When the medics arrived, they had to pry my door open to get me out. While the medics were putting me on their stretcher, my daughter said a lady walked over to her and asked if her mother had been "driving the black Jaguar? My daughter replied "Yes". The lady said her name was Mimi, and she told my daughter that I would be all right. She also told my daughter she was with me and that I would be all right.

If your mother doesn't stay calm, give her this tea. It will calm her down, she loves tea. My daughter got to the hospital and after making sure I was doing fine and stable in the emergency room, she began to tell me about the lady named Mimi who had given me some tea. She also told me that Mimi said I was with her and you were going to an interview; I asked my daughter "Who are you talking about"? I was by myself because I was going to my interview and you don't take people with you on an interview. She then said "The lady knew you mom". She knew the color of your car; she said how nice you were and everything; she spoke very nicely about you and said she was with you. After she finished talking about you, she gave me the tea. I thanked her for the tea and went back to answer questions for the police who were on the scene. My daughter asked her husband, "Where did the lady go"? He said he didn't see her anymore after she gave us the instruction to give to your mom. She was gone, but I have the tea she left with me. She said you must stay calm.

Angels, Angels, Angels
Watch Over You

How do you feel when you know that there is someone watching you day and night? It may be your mother, your father, the police, your wife, your husband, or your children. You know it is possible that this could be true, but as we know, the person watching will get tired after a while, and will take a break. So soon, they may just stop watching you if there is nothing going on that they are interested in. They will leave you alone. However, do you know who is always and forever watching over you? Jesus and His heavenly angels. They are always there as it is written in the Bible. 1 Corinthians 4-9 teaches us that the angels are watching over us. We must believe what the Bible says about them. Let me tell you what happened to me one night.

I went to church on a Saturday night to a wedding anniversary service for my Bishop and his wife. I enjoyed the service with plenty of good gospel singing. There were two groups singing great songs of praise that made us clap our hands and stomp our feet. The praise dancers were just magnificent, and there were mime dancers from a visiting church. The dancers were very anointed. After their performances, all we had to do was to honor the honorees and go home, you know "God is good".

"Seek and find the promised one -Jesus"

After I had to drop my husband off to work, I went home to relax for the night. My sister called to see how the service was and to make sure I got home safely. I told her that I was fine but a little tired. We continued to talk for a few more minutes. She told me to "get some rest and that she would talk to me tomorrow after church".

I started to say my prayers for the night, but all of a sudden I began to slur my words. I began to pray and yelled out "Help me, help me, help me!" The phone rang, and it was my husband calling me, the first thing he said was "Honey, you called me", I thought you would be sleep by now is everything ok? He began to ask me "What's wrong? What's wrong"? I could hardly talk, I told him that I didn't call him and that I hadn't picked up the phone to call anyone. I just got sick; I could not even talk for about two minutes", my husband said, "yes you did, I'm looking at the number right here on my cell phone". He said the call came in at 2:01 a.m., I am looking at it. I went on to explain to him just what was going on, I remembered what the Bible said in 1 Corinthians 4-9; that angels watch us also to guard over us, to protect us, to ward off hurt, harm or danger. The angel was there to help me and to contact my husband to let him know that I was in trouble and that I needed help right away.

"Seek and find the promised one Jesus"

By his quick response, he called my daughter to get the ambulance for me. The ambulance came and I was taken to the hospital with Jesus and his Angels being there with me. Jesus healing power and helping hands of the doctors and nurses. I am back after a few days in the hospital. I'm at home healed and recovering.

Believe me, I thanked God for God being God all by himself. I thank God for his son Jesus and I thank God for his Angels, His Heavenly Host of Angels who are with us to obey the commands of Jesus Christ.

Saints, stay saved and those of you that are not saved, you better get saved and filled with the Holy Ghost because you just don't know just how quickly you could be gone. You could say it could have been the other way. Even if you say it could have been the other way, you would want to know that you are saved and filled with the Holy Ghost and gone to a better place called Heaven. That is what my Bishop taught us for years- get saved;

stay saved and filled up. Stay in the word (the Bible) and live a life for Jesus Christ.

"Seek and find the promised one Jesus"

The devil is always present! For example, you go home and you are so stressed or tired, you lay down even though you know you need to pray, but you put if off and say I'm going to get up in a minute and pray but you don't! The devil also heard you so the Lord sent his angel to stand by you all night and watch over you, to ward off all hurt, harm and dangers.

But sometimes people give the devil more credit than he deserves by talking about what he made them do and what he did to them. Instead, we should give that time and praise to the good Lord; about how good the Lord is and his angels that watch over us all day and night while we go about our day and sleep at night. We should be thankful God for his Angels and his mercy and grace.

Angels are encamped around you all the time.

Angel are messengers sent by God to protect you.

Angels in Heaven are sent to comfort you.

My Angel's name was Mimi.

A Son's Prayer

Most holy righteous one, the son of God, my protection, my healer, my Savior; one who sits high and looks low. I praise Your name for who You are. Thank you for your grace and mercy. I thank you and your Angels for protecting my son from hurt, harm and death. I thank you for not even a broken bone after he fell off his motorcycle with a stroke on his right side and after having slid a half block and ended up under a cab, and the cab didn't move and run over him. Lord, I thank you, Lord I know You said that You would send angels to protect and watch over us. Jesus you did just what you said you would do.

Amen

Angels Appeared

Matthew 1-20: angels appeared to them

Abraham, Lot, Jacob and others they had no problem in recognizing the angels when God allowed the angels to appear and manifest themselves in the physical form.

Genesis 32: 1-2: Jacob was on his way and the Angels appeared and he saw them and said, "This is God's host".

Genesis 3-24: The Cherubim's were the first of the angels that God spoke of. He sent the Cherubim's down to watch over the tree of life so that Adam and Eve could not eat from the tree again for God had cast them out of the garden. His Cherubim's and a flaming sword that turned every way, were placed to keep the way of the tree of life.

God commanded the construction of the Ark of Covenant. He asked the builders to make two Cherubims of gold and put one on each end of the mercy seat and place them facing each other with their wings stretched out to cover the mercy seat. Exodus 25:18-19.

Cherubims are associated with the Glory of God... 1st Sam. 4-4, Isaiah 37: 15-16-17

The birth of Jesus was announced by the Great Angel Gabriel

The Cherubims are always at the throne of God. They are at His every call. They are all around Him; they are His honor guards.

Acts 1-10, the angels told the disciple that the same way they see Jesus go up to heaven is the same way He will return. The two angels in white told the disciples that as they stood watching Him ascend up to heaven.

Angel's are Called

Angels are differentiated by several different names, but in Hebrews 1:14, the Bible refers to them as ministering spirits without physical bodies, but they might take on physical bodies when appointed by God to do so, to perform special task by God.

Can Angels Reproduce?

No, angels cannot reproduce because God didn't give them the ability to reproduce and they do not marry nor are they given in marriage. (Mark 12:24 and 25:26)

Angels Brought the Law

Ten thousand angels came down on Mount Sinai to confirm the Holy presence of god as He gave the Law of Moses. (Deuteromary 33:1-3). The presence of the angels were so strong the earthquake shook the mountains. Moses was amazed at the presence of the heavenly host that attended; just think of angels everywhere on that mountain to honor their God, the Father out of the Angelic Hosts. There was a trumpet to announce the presence of God, the whole mountain came alive, the people were over joyed at the visitation of the Angelic Host of heavenly beings.

Reflections

Reflections

_____

_____

_____

_____

_____

_____

_____

_____

_____

_____

_____

Reflections

_____

_____

_____

_____

_____

_____

_____

_____

_____

_____

Chapter 5

Angels Appeared

The angels always travel with God; they are His secret agents.

Matthew 28:2-6

The angel was there to roll the stone away, and he sat upon it. The guard was left in such a terrified state that they became and looked like dead men. The angels spoke to the women who had come looking for the body of Jesus and said "Do not be afraid for He has risen".

A Daughter's Prayer

Lord Jesus, I glorify Your name; I honor you Jesus; I thank you Lord for being God all by Yourself. I thank you Jesus for my daughter. I thank you for saving her at an early age, and I thank you for all the right people being in place during her admittance into the hospital, from the doctors to the nurses to the paramedics and other employees. Your guardian angels that stood watch over her both day and night, I praise your name Jesus. I thank you for speaking and telling me to go back home so that I could get the phone call. If You had not spoken to me, I would not have been there. Lord I thank you for You for your grace and mercy.

Amen

I Saw, Now I See

I've been going to church for a long time, I
mean many years. I was raised in a Christian
household, with a mother and father who were
God fearing parents. There were 13 children, a
dog, a cat and even a pet pig, we were a family
that ate and prayed together. I say that to say
this, we believe in God and his Angels'. I grew
up in a Baptist church but later started going to
the Holiness church because I liked how they
taught the Bible and explained it (the Word)
to you. I was baptized and filled with the Holy
Spirit since I have been going to this church. I
have seen people give their life to Christ and get
filled with the Holy Spirit, I've seen people get
healed and delivered since I've been attending
this wonderful church. The Bishop and his wife
are very anointed, the Bishop is a man you could
talk to if you had a problem; his wife is very
quiet, but she's a praying woman of God. She's
always by her husband's side, as I grew from
being a babe in Christ up to being a saint, a wife
that loves the Lord. I also moved to become a
Deaconess, an intercessor, and a member of
our anointed senior choir for 32 years. God is
so good; I saw how the Lord just kept working

things out for me. Now I see the plan for my life, the road I must take and that is to keep his word and love the Lord with all my heart, mind and soul because Jesus is the only way.

Angels describes as in the appearance of man.

Ezekiel 10-8; 40-5; 40:6-7

Daniel 5-5; 8-16; 8-17

The Lord of Host Heavenly attendance

Exodus 11-1; 12-40; 41-42

1Samuel 1:3-11; 4-4; 16:1-17-45

2 Kings 3:14-15; 19:31-33

1 Kings 18-15; 19-10; 10-14

1 Chronicles 11-19; 17-17

Angels Heavenly Host (Division of God's Army)

Genesis 2-1; 32-2

Joshua 5:13-15

1 Kings 22:19-20

2 Kings 21:3-5

Daniel 8:10-12

Isaiah 14:4-6; 17-3; 18:6-7; 22:4-5

Haggai 2:4-7

Acts 7:53-54

Galatians 3:18-19

Colossians 2:18-20

1 Peter 1:12-14; 3:22-24

2 Peter 2-4; 2:11-12

1 Timothy 3:15-17; 5:21-23

2 Thessalonians 1:6-8

Matthew 4:6-13; 13:38-42; 2:1-3; 22:30-31; 24:30-36; 25:30-32; 25:40-41; 26:52-54;

Luke 12:8-10; 16:22-23; 20:35-36; 24:23-24

Mark 1:13-15; 12:24-25; 13:27-33

Galatians 13:19-20

Revelation 5:11-12; 7:1-11; 8:2-13; 13:9-16; 12:7-9; 15:1-8; 17:1-3; 21:9-12

John 1-51; 20:12-14

Romans 8:37-39

Acts 5:19-20; 6-15; 7:30-31; 10:7-23; 12:8-23; 27:22-23, 27-24

Job 38:4-7; 32-5

Nehemiah 9-6

Psalms 103:18-20; 19-1; 91-11; 104:4-7

1Timothy 6:13-14

2 Corinthians 12:2-3; 3:6-7

Ezekiel 28:14-16; 10:9-17

Jude 5:6-9

Matthew 24-1; 25:41-42; 1:17-19; 2:13-15

Revelation 4:11-13; 13:24-30; 13-43; 3-1; 4:1-6; 22-8; 2-7; 12:7-9; 4-19

1 Kings 19:5-7

Matthew 13:41-42; 28:2-4

Responsive Reading

Joshua 5:12-14

Zechariah 1:11-15

Exodus 2:1-3; 25-20; 13-22; 1-23; 5-20

Revelation 4:5-7; 3:1-2; 1:5-8

Psalms 91-11

Daniel 3-28

Mark 12-25

John 4-5; 16-21; 6:63-64; 1:1-15

Genesis 1:1-17; 18:14-15; 3:15-24

Acts 6:30-32; 1:8-12

1 Kings 15-16; 18-19

Numbers 21-1; 22:21-33

James 2:18-19

Isaiah 6:2-3

Recommended Reading

Angel- The Greek word Aggelos means messenger, one who was sent by God to deliver tidings.

1 Samuel 29: 9-10

2 Samuel 14:16-17, 20-21, 24:16 17-18

Luke 1:10 11-12, 18:19-28, 2:10-21, 22:24

Revelation 12:6-10, 9:1-2-3, 10:7-8-9

Hosea 12:4-5

Matthew 1:20-21, 2:13-28, 28:2-3-4-5

Well, I guess everyone believes in angels to a certain extent, and that everyone has a guardian angel. It is a warm feeling to know that there is always a Godly presence watching over you day and night. I count it an honor to have them watching over me.

Every day I must press my way through. Press. Press. I must press my way through, I can't give up now because God has something waiting for me for all the tears and for enduring everything that I have gone through. God has got something waiting for me.

For the Lord is good and his mercy is everlasting and his truth endures to all generation.

Psalms 24:4-5

One thing I have desired of the Lord is that I seek that I may dwell in the house of the Lord all the days of my life, to behold the beauty of the Lord and to inquire in his temple for in the time of trouble. He shall hide me in his pavilion in the secret place of his tabernacle he shall hide me; he shall set me high upon a rock.

Psalms 27:3

For God is our God forever and ever; he will be our guide even unto death. Psalms 4-14

There shall no evil befall thee, neither shall any plague come nigh thy dwelling for he shall give his angels charge over thee to keep thee in all thy ways.

Psalms 91:10-12

For I will restore health unto thee and I will heal thee of thy wounds, saith the Lord.

Jeremiah 30:17

Questions and Answers

1. Whom do you think called my husband?

    _____

    _____

2. Do you believe angels are here to watch over us?

    _____

    _____

3. Conduct research on Angels and find out how fast they can travel from heaven to earth and around the earth at God's command.

    _____

    _____

4. Can Jesus heal instantly?

    _____

    _____

Questions and Answers

5. Can Jesus do anything, but fail?

_____

_____

6. What benefits do you get from being loved?

_____

_____

7. How often should you pray?

_____

_____

8. How should you pray?

_____

_____

9. How many heavens are there?

_____

_____

10. Which heaven does God and His angels reside?

_____

_____

11. When did you become a born again Christian?

_____

_____

Different Names of God

1. Abba Father

2. All Mighty God

3. Ancient of Days

4. Beautiful Crown

5. Consuming Fire

Different Names of God

6. Counselor

7. Creator

8. Crown of Glory

9. Deliverer

10. Dwelling Place

Different Names of God

11.   Doctor

12.   Descendent

13.   Door

14.   Eternal Father

15.   Eternal Life

Different Names of God

16. Everlasting Father

17. Everlasting Light

18. First Begotten

19. Faithful

20. God With Us

Different Names of God

21. High Priest

22. Heir of All Things

23. Holy

24. Hope of glory

25. I Am

Different Names of God

26. Image of God

27. Immanuel

28. Instructor

29. Jesus

30. Jesus Christ

Different Names of God

31. Jesus of Galilee

32. Jesus of Nazareth

33. Just Man

34. King

35. King of Kings

Different Names of God

36. King of The Jews

37. Lamb of God

38. Life

39. Lord

40. Lord Jesus

Different Names of God

41. Lord Of Lords

42. Man Of Sorrows

43. Master

44. Mediator

45. Mighty God

Different Names of God

46. Messiah

47. Nazarene

48. Omega

49. Only Begotten son

50. Only Son

Different Names of God

51.   Physician

52.   Prince

53.   Prophet

54.   Quickening Spirit

55.   Redeemer

Different Names of God

56. Righteous

57. Saviour

58. Shepherd

59. Son Of Man

60. Teacher

Different Names of God

61. True Vine

62. True God

63. Truth

64. Umpire

65. Way

Different Names of God

66. Wittiness

67. Wonderful Counselor

68. Word of God

69. Word

70. Young Man of Exalted

Special Thanks

To My Family and Friends

Minister Altheria Jones

Tina Leonard